Towards Light

Also by Sarah Day

A Hunger To Be Less Serious (1987)
A Madder Dance (1992)
Quickening (1996)
New and Selected Poems (2002) UK
The Ship (2004)
Grass Notes (2009)
Tempo (2013)

Towards Light
& Other Poems

Sarah Day

PUNCHER & WATTMANN

First published in 2018

Published by Puncher and Wattmann
PO Box 441
Glebe NSW 2037
http://www.puncherandwattmann.com
puncherandwattmann@bigpond.com

National Library of Australia
Cataloguing-in-Publication entry:

Day, Sarah
Towards Light & Other Poems

ISBN 9781925780024
I. Title.
A821.3

Cover design by Gordon Harrison-Williams

This project has been assisted by the Australian Government through the Australia Council, its arts funding and advisory body.

Australian Government

Australia Council
for the Arts

Contents

IV

V

Introduction

Sarah Day looks closely, and considers carefully what she sees, what is experienced, what is lost — she 'is not insensible to change' any more than the world itself is — and also what is to be cherished. It is a highly tuned work of deep awareness, looking at surfaces and what lies beneath them — of the earth, of the made, of migration, of home and distance, of the costs of presence, of mortality, of loss, and also of beauty. It's further evidence of the essential way of seeing that Day offers us in her skillfully honed and calibrated poetry of *being* — and the difficulties, contradictions and consequences of watching the world unfold. Ultimately, it is a collection that expresses her belief in people and nature.

John Kinsella

I

Fe

Magnetic north is always on the move,
looping its slow deep subterranean loops
around true north which it eludes
like an errant partner in an Arctic dance. Whoops –
gliding now at forty k per year from Canada
towards Siberia like a planchette on a Ouija –
anyone would think these shifts might derange
a home-bound salmon and rearrange
the map for pigeon, turtle, snow goose
or the coded alphabet inside the honey bee
dance; it all seems set to confuse
but fails. Blood hears more than its own euphony
as the sliding behemoth in fits and starts
quietly adjusts our compasses, our hearts.

Fog

Lake St Clair, Tasmania

Picture a deep lake,
wild forests sloping steeply
to the shores, mountain peaks
where waters bend out of sight
behind the distant headland.

Now, erase the scene with fog,
thick fog, so that before you
there is neither land nor lake nor sky,
there is just a jetty to which
a small, green ferryboat is tied

floating on pigeon-grey air.
Imagine the stillness −
nothing moves or whispers.
Great black boulders
with their rings of lichen also float.

For a moment the sun
and its watery rainbow-ringed
companion glow dimly through
the fog. Erase them too −
the ferryman needs to be undistracted

as he unhooks the painter
and reverses a quiet arc,
your last glimpse of him
in profile, his dark cap
pulled low over his ears,

an upright silhouette at the wheel,
the little prow nose-up, optimistic.
Man, ferry, empty seats,
vanishing into the vacuum.
Gone, before you can draw breath,

leaving only this high definition
concrete jetty with its rusting pillars
and yellow parallel lines like a highway's
bolting towards the blank unknown.
And the mute pulse in the grey white fog

of an engine going somewhere.
Think of him, the ferryman,
if he were ever there at all
on the illusory lake,
his implacable blindness.

St Anthony Preaches to the Fishes

(Azulejo, Lisbon)

The ignorant cluster on the humpback bridge,
unaware that the stone arches below form
three perfect ovals with the mirror image in the water,
and that light passes lucidly under their heavy feet.

In his monk's robe and sandals,
on the river bank, Saint Anthony
must have wondered as the fish broke
the waters in a splash of sequined scale

and droplets from the deep,
straining on their tails as one,
the little fishes to the front, the great fishes
of the sea listening from the distance beyond.

In his demeanour
neither hubris, nor madness nor despair;
he is hitching up his skirts to avoid tripping.
He has something to tell.

His words, fallen on deaf ears,
have found the eager faces of the fish.
His words fly upwards too, on wings
of numerous indeterminate birds.

I see now how the arced frame of the blue
and white tiled tableau repeats the arches
of the bridge, so that the whole metaphor
of foolishness becomes a tunnel into light.

Sea Ice

The slowly setting sun lights up the cracks
in sea ice. An aerial view may show
that what appears a solid mass reacts –

is not insensible to change. The facts
are obfuscated, though
the slowly setting sun lights up the widening cracks.

Frazil-ice is granular and lacks
a crust: the heft and turbulence below
stirs up a slush; the solid mass reacts

as now the waterline, like wax,
recedes, yields up the pieces of the self below.
The slowly setting sun lights up the cracks;

the mind, like salt encased in ice, refracts;
less light reflected into space – who knows
how a solid mass of white reacts?

This state of dissolution now enacts
a breaking up of everything. Green and low
the slowly setting sun lights up the cracks
and what appears a solid mass reacts.

Knocklofty

Annihilating all that's made
To a green thought in a green shade
                    Marvell

The asphalt ends, the road becomes
a gravel track,
stillness not so much descends
as waits where houses end;

the last power line, the last dog's bark,
white traffic noise dissolves;
you leave behind the open sky
to step beneath a canopy

into a tree light atrium
in which breeze and mind are hushed;
bees drone at distant height
disturb the shape of air in each tree's form,

the easy smell of moss and rotting leaf
the pep and clarity of eucalyptus oil;
the heartbeat slows and pays attention to
the single notes the small birds sing.

Upwards, smooth trunks draw the eye,
clouds and ravens fly
above the gully's aviary
like someone else's thoughts;

through a green lens, the fractal calm
of fern and wattle leaf, the pattern too
of lichen on sandstone like hidden quolls.
You disappear in a place like this

where time unfolds and spreads
itself through air and light,
each sense responds to this essential love,
the green gauze stills the heart, the eye.

Reservoir

Sleeping in its brick tabernacle
the still water is like an ear or radar dish
attuned to distant pulse. Incurious,
we've walked forever to school and work
past locked gates. The saw tooth roof
gives nothing away but scission with sky
and though the key-hole draws the eye, the pupil
contracts. Inside, a herringbone of oak beams
and rafters hovers over the water's weight
and repose. It is like opening a door
and finding the room full of water.
Beyond the inscrutable iron fence
the street's steep uphill/ downhill zeal;
urban windows; the domestic race
of breakfast, phones and life and birth and death.
Inside this null and void this leave no trace
the morning sun has picked the lock,
entering through a gable's little porthole,
bending light with its oblique know-how.

Wooden Horse

on your crude wooden sled,
you were once – a broom,
a length of rope,
a handful of off-cuts, two screws
and eight three inch nails.
You are not quite symmetrical –
one rocker pine, one hardwood,
and your plank torso is bevelled
more on the left than the right.
Your hard round eye has been drilled
right through your plank face;
from above, this gives you a bright
dark vacancy. To a child
this might lend perspicacity
(squatting and peering,
I can see the evening ocean
through your clear gaze);
the same bit bore the hole
for the dowel handle that impales
your jaw; your profile is not equine,
more Border Leicester.
Your crimped rope tail and mane
have been mere tufts of stubble
like nibbled wallaby grass
since you first came our way.
Your broom legs are *so* straight,
slender as a racehorse's;
I forgot to say
that there is some pathos
about your routered mouth,

and its odd slope of forbearance.
Your broom neck leans forward
towards the future. I suspect
you never boasted a coat of paint;
nowadays you are so weathered
you might be made of driftwood –
a horse of the sea.
Your balance is exact,
the elipse of each crude arc
rocker knows to baulk
just before the tipping point.
Earless, eyeless yet not blind,
bereft of mane and tail,
you are steadfast, gazing
through that vacant eye
to east and west,
seeing not, in your long life,
that children grow old,
but how, from each tide,
rolls the continuum of each wave.

Jetty

As pragmatic
as a wooden jetty may be

bolted to fact and need
with post and bollard

and plank, a jetty is also
a transcendentalist

believing democratically
that we may all walk over

water toward a cool horizon,
the line of thought

poised above the plane
across a sea of white horses

or an even-tempered
windless millpond.

The Reader

Effigy of Eleanor of Aquitaine, Fontevrault, 12c.

Here's a consummate work of love
in limestone. The way the wimple
tenderly surrounds her face;
the modest crown, the ease and grace
with which her long smooth hands
support her book upon her chest,
the angle of the elbow, and the wrist.
But where the sculptor's care is felt
the most is in the way they understand
resistance, yield, the pillow
gently giving way beneath the head
and neck; beneath the buckled belt
the gathered cloth, the belly's rise;
the crease where hip and elbow
press upon the bed. The strap that ties
the cobalt shawl held taut across
her collarbone, the shawl itself pinned by
the corner of the book against her breast;
the all-important book to which the eye
returns and finds sublime; the cross
waves of her dress's fanning pleats.
Her body's grace and weight,
a purity that touches earth where
the book rests on her fingertips;
devotion links rock to love and air.
If it were needed, here in stone's
time's living proof of the loving heart,
if not for the subject, then the art.

Towards Light

I whisper something to you
about the humility of the church window, the way the lower third
opens, like a kitchen window, on a simple casement hinge;
Spanish mission you murmur in the dimness, without turning
from the fado singer at the altar. We're inside an antipodean
      Vermeer –
in the sepia voice and reflected light and in the simple geometry
of the half circle in the top third of the window frame.

Without the assurance of the senses, what is reason?
The movement of the eye towards light stirs such promise:
a garden path towards the morning sun through silhouette
of fig, grevillea and loquat leaf. Or light on the Southern Ocean
glimpsed through aperture of tea-tree corridor;
light permeates shadow, a camera obscura. The ocean's spaciousness
enters the prickly bower.

The light at the end of the tunnel's a familiar trope
for hope or faith or birth and death.
The transparency of shadow –the way light bounces through,
illuminates a dogwood leaf, a cherry plum;
unsentimental, this walking towards light.
Not the arrival, not the blaze of daylight beyond the portal
out of the dark on the downhill track to the foaming swell,

but the momentary equilibrium, parenthesis of arching tree-light.
The fado singer in the church sings for what is past and gone:
a melancholy longing in the minor key,
but the light from the window transports us
forwards in time. Sometimes the dead come back to life

and speak of avenues to light.
The beautiful is limited but the sublime is infinite,

some hunger's met in the threshold –
this elation in light's diffusion,
the way everything leads
in a forest path overhung with banksia
or a shimmering head-high symphony of xanthorrhoea,
to the vanishing point where light will expand,
where light wants the eye to go.

Overcoat

And you know, there is no such thing as society,
there are individual men and women. And there are families:
Margaret Thatcher

He took out his wallet
to fix up the bill while she examined
the Royal Guide Dogs puppy bank
at the other end of the counter,
looking for the slot in which to press
her two dollar coin.
They appeared in the half-lit waiting room
of the doctor's surgery
as if they'd walked off an extras scene
in a Second World War film or, as if they'd just
walked out of my childhood
– they'd have been old fashioned then –
in the nineteen sixties.
Some things endure
like the coarse woollen coats
this wife and husband wore
that belonged to a former time.
Cut and stitched and lined to last –
a sort of life assurance.

They had entered
from the dark corridor behind,
nodding a greeting to each and every person
waiting, even the girl on her mobile phone
talking angrily to the window glass
as if her mother, to whom she remonstrated,
was on the other side out there on the street.

They entered the room
and nodded —
she almost bobbed her good will
to the eye of each who'd return it,
and to those who didn't.
We were somehow,
even the girl on the phone,
all brought together in their greeting.

He took out his wallet,
while she traced her two-dollar coin down
the slope of the dog's polymer neck,
around its pedestal,
turned and smiled. Tried the crown
and the back of the head, giggled like a girl,
finding no slot
in which to drop her money.
Their brown overcoats were waisted,
and belted, with broad lapels and double breast.
How long had they worn them?
Some sixty, seventy years?
A coat, back then,
was a coat for life, like a couch. It saw you out.

They had the young faces
of those who grow up in cold countries
and a tone of collective thinking
in their demeanour; in their salutation;
in their overcoats and hard worn leather shoes;
in their courtesy.
They belonged to a generation
for whom buying meant a thing had broken
or worn beyond repair…

...The bill paid, the coin having found its way

they bade us all farewell,

walked out into the windy street

and yellowing light

with the rest of the dwindling numbers

of an age undisposed to leave one another alone.

II

Europe

June, 2016

The flight path on the screen
across the aisle is a green line
joining the dots from Manchester
through Amsterdam, Bucharest,
now Istanbul, now Baghdad.
Far below us the Tigris River seeps
like history from the Taurus Mountains.
Europe is an idea not a market
the French president is saying
on BBC World News though tomorrow
most news will be of stock market
fears, the depression of investment.
The prime minister of the UK
has just resigned, affirming
in his final words, as if at a funeral,
his love for his country.
The little plane on the map
is towing the bright green line
to the dot that is Basra.
Najur the Indian boy is four years old;
he offers me his crisps,
his blanket, his Scooby Doo show
on TV – everything he has.
He counts twenty in English,
then in Hindi and calls me Aunty
tucking his mother's and my knees
under his blanket.
The plastic fold out table is littered
with plastic cups and plastic cutlery.

I think of Auden,
from his dive on 52nd Street
watching his world unfold.
An idea, not a market,
yet here, on screen, is the stock exchange
and the pound has plummeted
taking with it the zloty, the rand,
the yuan, the peso as well as
the CAC and the DAX.
Wales is celebrating, Scotland angry.
Cameron wants a slow separation,
Europe moots a quick divorce.
There are already ruptures
between neighbours and brothers.
On Wigan main road young men fight
and shout; the old men in their forties
sit, as usual, outside the council flats
to talk and smoke.
The young men want to punch
and punch the living daylights
out of everything. Their knuckles itch
for cheek and jaw;
shoppers and schoolchildren
skirt a broad arc around them.
London and the universities
vote Remain; the estates
and the ex-miners and workers
chorus Leave. They are the ruthless
propagandists' easy victory.
Hope? smiled the Dalai Lama,
the union of Europe
after centuries of bloodshed,
has given me much hope

in the twentieth century.
The Etihad Box screens interviews
with Germany, China, Japan
and Singapore. A wooden block
has been slid from the foundations
of the tower. The idea curls at the edges
like a map to a flame.
The E Box informs us we are flying
at an altitude of 37,000 feet;
at a ground speed of 896k per hour;
outside the air is minus forty degrees.
Basra passes beneath us.
The altered reality above,
beyond range of the human ear,
is tracking on radar somewhere below.
On the flight map Europe's green
gives way to a vast arid white.
Beneath the screen's abstraction
white emits crowds
who hold hopes for the green
where there is water to drink,
where food grows, where fear may abate.
Shutters are drawn against the night;
sleeping heads bump in unison
against their rests as the Airbus,
like a great edifice, catapulting
far above the clouds,
jostles and swoops in the jet-stream.
BBC World News presenter, a latter day
Tacitus watching Rome burn,
maintains her commentary.
Across Manchester's blue sky
jet planes' condensation trails

weave a hectic plaid
and in the void a myriad glinting
flight-paths on screens join dots to dots.

Dunes

The suburban bus route
elicits in its rider
a mood of compliance
while it finds the longest distance
possible between two points,
allowing that time is expendable,
that mangrove swamps, ti-tree forests
and wild coasts become sub-divisions
with names like Anna Bay, Corlette.
Everything happens in slow motion,
each passing sign a long call
for attention: Subway Drive-Thru;
Baylife Church; Laser Skirmish;
Spectrum Church School and Café.
At a point which could be
half-way, the bus pulls in beside
Putters Mini Golf
and Clay Target Shooting
on a gravel shoulder
across from a boggy farm
that wants to be marsh land.
The engine cuts. One or two people
continue to talk about the health
problems of someone they know,
then stop. The driver methodically
closes and locks his black change box,
takes his lunch in its paper bag,
folds his beaded seat comforter
under his arm and leaves to speak
to the uniformed man in the white ute

who will become our driver
when they have both done chatting
and nodding and passing the time of day.
In rear windows the blank passivity of children
is reflected. Then, another curbed roundabout,
another drained swamp, another turn-off
from the destination through land
just cleared of forest and koala,
now decorated with surveyors' pegs.
A derelict mess drifts by
of concrete holiday apartments that
the inexorable dunes are repossessing;
and then another Toy-Town retail centre
with its improbable pink spire
and its singular icons:
the Giant Skittle, the Golden Arches.

big punchbowl

Freycinet Peninsula

if there is no one to welcome us
to this country
with its ringing cicadas and water ribbon,
grass frogs syncopating in its freshwater crucible,
then we come here unwelcomed

if there is no one to welcome us
to this lagoon country
where the lone swan trails its single cygnet
beneath the loving gaze of the sea eagle
her hungry young at home in their tower of sticks,
then we have come here unwelcomed

if there is no one to welcome us
to this shore
where we have left tracks in the pristine glasswort,
then we come here unwelcomed

there is the time it will take
for each string of salt pearls to unbend
inside the shadow of our footprints;
there is also the deep prehistory
of swamp memory and there are the present owners
of this house we have entered unbidden

if there is no one to welcome us
to this forest country
in whose unfading patience the grass trees shiver,
then we have come here unwelcomed.

Empire

1967

A cord and ring pulled down the Empire map
to conceal the blackboard's daily spelling list,
the teacher's bamboo pointer tapped
and sketched the outline
of the raspberry pink that blotched The World.
I sat up straight and felt, while not her pride,
complacent ease, a sense of being on the winning side.

The school bus loped along the gravel road
that sometimes crumbled in a rising tide,
crossed the wooden bridge across the silted
estuary and passed, without a backward look
from anyone, the dark stone monument
to those who first set foot from European boats.
The linking in my child's mind of flags, red coats,

guns, with the dusky scrub and Casuarina slopes
through which we wound our journey home
was as remote in time as the Second World War
that finished little more than twenty years before.
The past gets closer as you age; I see now that then
just two long lives divided me from when
those sails enthralled the river and the silent, wary bush.

At school, in wooden rows, we practised
doublethink, the art of knowing contradictory
principles to be true. 'Thou shalt not steal':
a man raised on the axioms of Rome
could walk into another's house, call it his own.

The boat, the monument, the map, the ring,
the pointing stick — we had a sense of everything

and nothing in the colonial spill of pink,
though Now and Then were easier to tell apart.
Today I find the future in the past,
the past inside the now that is both fleeting
and continuous. Maps… stories… I'm more wary of
the shifting palimpsest of truths, the fanatic tides,
the celluloid transparencies, the overlaying slides.

Middens, Tasmania

The presence of the past lies on the river-
banks, the island coasts and estuaries:
the recent past, and all that came before.
The past's a state of mind here

of confrontation and avoidance,
in the crunch of mussel underfoot,
the powdered lime and remnant scallop
crimps in tell-tale Georgian mortar.

Here, what's come before defines with
keenness of oyster shell, detail of fish bone,
honed in sea light as today's continuum
of women drawing molluscs from the shallows

while above millennia of human history
jets fly like short-lived gnats.

III

Scissors

With silver scissors from a bag of toothbrush, flannel, soap, I snip along a radius from the pursed mouth of the wombat's pouch. Her blood stopped running hours ago. A cold wind blows off the plateau; the country road is empty. Bush exhales its morning scent of eucalyptus. Her thick flesh cuts reluctantly; I hear its rubbery resistance. Her baby is curled in its bed. It takes two to lift the mother's great weight off the gravel and into the long grass where the quolls and ravens will soon find her. Against a child's warm heartbeat, the young wombat stirs to life from cold's numb slumber. We turn on the ignition, facing south. A sad story with a happy ending though the dumb stones in the paddocks will call out after us in anger and sorrow.

Eastern Curlew

A contagion like telepathy
ruffles the flock,
shuddering with altered light
and wind, a pectoral yearning
for the dot to dot of stars
and the mind's magnet drawn
to the Arctic. We lift,
we float and feather and fan
back to Earth. And lift and float again
our slow rehearsal on the shore.
Some call it *Zugunruhe* –
this restlessness to move – our lust-
longing for the breeding grounds
of Russia, China and Siberia.
We've done with mud dibbling
day and night, dispensed for now
with lagoon and sand flat months,
the serenity of sea grass.
We're leaving at nightfall,
the long haul North calls.
No one has signalled
yet we are all of one mind
and we are all rehearsing:
lifting, fanning, floating,
chatting about anything but
the Journey and the Gobi Desert gold
of The Yellow Sea half way
glinting and shrinking –
no longer crab rich in bog and marsh,
more road and wall now and human

tower, putrid leaks and pestilence.
We curlews fossick clean sand,
we probe salt clean mud
for limpid life, we are not
sludge siphons, and the psychedelia
of plastic bits that lure the eye
twists the guts. Some friends turn back,
resolved to make Summer of Winter,
others will slacken from the flyway
with hunger over a dark sea.
Pulled by memory, hope
and this deep ancestral ache
the rest of us who leave
this ancient continent tonight
will set our compass
for Kamchatka, Amur....

Peacock Spider

Will she take me for a mate
or make a meal of me?
If I called out for help
who'd hear?
This is the dance of the Dead,
the Loving, and the Living –
the bush shrunk in its rustle
and bird talk to dumb suspense,
an invisible audience
to our theatre in the round
played on twig and leaf.
My uncertain semaphore
of SOS... OS, spells Fear, Desire,
her scalding eyes a row
of emeralds on a ring.
The mantra's *best foot forward*
while this iridescent blue and orange
might just hold the key...
She never takes her eyes off mine.
Ablaze, I dance
as though my life depends on it.
In my own eyes she'll read
Terror, Ecstasy, sheer Curiosity,
as she affects a brown neutrality,
a robe of ordinariness.
I maintain the gaze –
a blink might be fatal.
These are my best moves.
And these! There's no tomorrow
in this rhythm and sway.

Love? Love!
Share the gum leaf stage with me;
love me, love me with your eyes of God.

Gannet

Call us experts
of mathematical precision,
of motion parallax
and high speed depth perception.
Admire the vatic eye inside
Egyptian kohl lined hieroglyphs.
Construct all the models you will
to test how an observer
might form a view of the world
at one location
yet use it at another.

And I will say how hunger fills a gap
when time stops in a breathless
break-neck streamlined plunge;
that the thrill of breaking
through water from air
is a conversion of mind and body
and that a snared fish, silver in the bill,
is a new idea of heaven, every time.

The Last Days

In the last days
of the big hen's life –
the best layer we ever had –
the bantam, who was a sixth her size
and nearly six times her age,
took up a vigil
beside the dying hen's head.
Silent, attentive without fuss,
she was there at daybreak
until dusk. For all I know,
she sat like a priest or a mother
or the good companion she was
through two long nights
on the straw at the head
of the large hen.
On the second day, the large hen
rested her head on the straw,
no longer having the strength
or will to hold it up,
her hen breaths gradually lightening.
We left them a little while like that
after the life finally expired.
An irony that of the two
the more robust should be the one
to sink down on the straw
and not get up. Her plumage
when I laid her in her grave
was burnished gold
in the evening light.
You can't help but wonder what goes on

in the mind of a small bereft bird
in the shadows of her tin house
at nightfall,
the stars in their brightness above.

A Chicken's Head

(Apologies to Miroslav Holub)

In it there are beetles and sesame seed
and a project
for a deep bed dust bath.

And there is
Sunlight
which shall be first
and the changing season
both of which are noticed in the pineal gland
behind the eyes
even in a life in a tin shed.
beneath fluorescence.

And there is
dandelion and groundsel
and borage and comfrey
as well as grass.

There is radar for movement
within the constant binary
of the right eye's near
and the left eye's far:

On a good day there is blue sky free of presentiment

But there are blind nights filled with rat scutter
cat glide and the silence of the barn owl's flight

There is the starry sky
And it just cannot be trimmed

I believe that   bliss   anxiety   peace   and   fear
inhabit the head of the chicken
like windy days and overcast days and brilliance,
that there is room too for the less elemental emotions
such as loyalty cunning   affection and pride

But that for shame, guilt, remorse
there is little space

I believe
that only what cannot be imagined
is a chicken's head

There is much promise
in a vision that numbers ultra violet
in its marvellous spectrum

Camp Ground. Early Morning.

In the shade of an angophora
an old bloke in a fisherman's hat
and his solemn wire-haired terrier
listen to a transistor's morning news.

Against an unbroken blue sky
Corellas wheel noisily with rapid wing beat
keeping the pink galahs quiet for a change.
The latter become statuesque observers
in the high branches of a scribble gum.

Like a movie sound-track magpies, out of sight,
are carolling a musical morning song.

Two children with sticks enact a slow-motion
martial art. The girl gets the worse of it and cries.

Another old bloke rides by on a rickety bicycle.
His thongs turn the pedals in slow time.

Pastel dressing gowns and slippers cross
the patchy lawn and concrete paths
back and forth to the amenities block.

A leisurely egalitarianism exists between camper,
terrier, doberman, adult, child, rosella.

Washing flaps from guy ropes.

Ibis cross the sky in formation.

Another dog, another camper (pink flowers
float like waterlilies on her green gown).

From its portable kennel under a palm
a mutt observes the goings on of camp grounds.

Blinds are still drawn in the *Winnebegos* ;
tent flaps are rolled down;
folding chairs and tables vacant.

A corgi-cross-jack russell trots by
like someone who has business to conduct.

On a circle of red canvas, bold white capitals read:

FIRE   HOSE   REEL

Apart from the many coloured number-plates,
camper and caravan brands, the occasional
name airbrushed in cursive on duco,
signs, logos and sell are absent.

Three black cockatoos glide by
trailing three long screeches like banners.
For a moment, they dispatch all birdlife,
even the corellas lie low. Lampooning
the rosellas, noisy mynahs are the first to return.

Taps drip. Currency is water,
a power pole, a rectangle of concrete
and a code number to the shower.
Currency is conversation, a neighbour's fish.

The couple who have been packing since dawn, buckle up.
Through your cabin window slot
Inspiration slides away in copperplate
with the slow acceleration of four-hundred horse-power.

Promises Promises

Rejoinder to Hardy's "He Never Expected Much"

High romance in neon
shapes the heart's luminous ideal;
Hollywood rebranded *Love*, now, somehow
Life lights up along a similar fluorescence.

What might Hardy's humble World
have said of instagram or advertising edicts
to feel the passion; reach for the stars,
the imperatives of every sell —

a house; a church; a fridge;
a university degree; a hopeful politician —
to follow those prismatic dreams
through sand-dunes and platitudes in four-wheel drives —

Neutral tinted haps and such?
— tsk World!
with your heavenly light, your understated tone
and muted promises.

Just now, a bantam singing
in a bath of dust beside me, tosses
with her claw and beak the powdered soil
between each feather, under each spread wing.

The barbarians

Because we cannot see eye to eye
we maintain a distance from the barbarians.
Their tongues and ours shape different words
for the country before us. We are aliens,

we have no point of common parlance,
between us words fall like stones.
We see a forest, a street or a bell-clear coast,
in their line of sight are development zones.

There's disjunction between what's seen
and what's named; we're mutually abstruse
confused, we lack a translator,
they do not speak our patois – bar, bar, bar.

Gut all the history, leave the façade
profit sheds its own light – bar, bar, bar.

Hinsby

Morning has swung to the north;
the sun now takes a sideways view
along the swell's long corrugations.
Beneath the water line light breaks
and shimmies on the seabed.
Lungs expand, exhale, as water
draws through sand, recedes;
the fracture on the cliff ahead
the swimmer's guiding pendulum.
Now the tow of sand, now sea,
now autumn's water light,
now the judicious sky. And now
like jellyfish across the green bay we drift
and undulate with the suck and sweep
of each wave's advance, each retreat.

Runaway

A fugitive budgie
in a democracy, or an empathy
of sparrows –

a sudden eddy
out of the blackberries
by the railway track

that is a ball of wing-beat
and sparrow twitter
dips, swoops, departs

leaving in its absence
an afterimage of aberrant
turquoise among grey chestnut.

Pastoral

The horse, one foreleg relaxed,
bows its head over the sleeping sheep.

*

Native hens with chicks
saunter and peck,

*

cattle egret punctuate the periphery.
Shadows from the stand of eucalypts

*

stretch half way up the hill.
Late autumn.

*

Skylarks whistle
their descending wonderment.

*

Further away a magpie sings
its five note riff – three times.

*

The dairy hums above the valley,
cows file along the profile of the hill.

*

Bull-rushes mirrored in the still water
of the dam frame the sky's oval brilliance.

*

The sheep wakes, lifts its Nubian profile.
The horse, off duty, turns ninety degrees

*

to look beyond salt-marsh to ocean,
easing the weight off one back leg

*

transfers the load forwards.
A falcon watches from a fence post.

*

Smoke drifts vertically from a distant chimney.
A kookaburra in an old gum tree

*

can contain itself no longer;
ravens incognito in the mass of macrocarpa

*

respond, indignant. Shorter than
the seeding head of dock

*

the native hens are slim dark pyramids.
An effect of light makes each appear one-eyed.

*

An Eastern Spinebill trills
Egypt! Egypt!

*

A car passes on the gravel road
from north to south.

*

Raven wings beat the air.
Alpha hen, on alert for falcon

*

beats a warning drum deep in her throat.
Another clan responds from far away.

*

The telegraph pole casts a shadow
like a candelabrum

*

on the corrugated roof of a shed.
The horse, who is lying down now,

*

stretches her neck to cough
once, twice, three times.

*

Her bass resonates across the paddock.
She lies flush with the earth

*

a long dark hump
on the curve of the hill

*

with her lump of a hip. It is now
the turn of the sheep with the sun on its face

*

to stand guard; the native hens
and their chicks gather round too,

*

to observe or to keep watch over
or to wonder at the sleeping horse.

Scale Model

Free Range Eggs says the sign
at the edge of the road.

And we see that, sure enough,
on the sward cut out of

the ancient forest that is
trying its hardest

to push back into the paddock,
is a small farmhouse

and some outhouses with wire
pens for the white chickens.

Against the backdrop of
the towering gum trees

that crowd at the fence line
the house looks smaller still.

The white hens with their red legs
and combs scratch and peck

like any other as if unaware of
or indifferent to the tall trees'

stand-over tactics. Nor do
they care if the whole scene

stands at the edge of an escarpment
down which colossal pipelines

plummet from the forest
to a tiny power station far below

where turbines guzzle
from the cataracts, and steel

transmission towers march away
into distance like cybermen.

Could you envy the hens their quest
for a blade of grass, an ear of cereal,

a glinting mote of quartzite
for a good strong shell?

In the Glass

In a pool of lamplight
in the dark house
the black print of the open book
knits the rows of its story.

The curtains are parted.
The window looks out
into the black of night.

The red ash, the blue gum,
the wide ocean, may
be out there somewhere.

A soft scratch, like a possum,
stirring to life in the eaves,
or a starling scuffling in the flue.

Upstairs, a shuffle –
the turning of a page,
then, downstairs,
the lightest ping

of a fingernail catching
the kettle's shiny image
of a little round room.

The words on the page
are rows of hieroglyphs.
There is an apparition in the glass –

a reader at a kitchen table
in a circle of light

and an orbiting bat
that flies too fast to be seen
except in reflection.

The window notes how
for an instant, the letters spiral
stroboscopic, from the page,
to rearrange the story.

Galicia

It's good to be somewhere
where a small field of corn
surrounded by four stone walls
is as much entitled as anybody
to a view, a waterside view,
of the Atlantic, or the wild head-
lands and pretty towns and ports
of the Costa da Morte.
Dry-stone walls run along
profile of rock and hill and field
to white beaches and rocky bays,
shielding from wind rows of young corn
and cabbage, as if a prime view
were just a place on earth for thrift
and periwinkle and clover
to exist alongside lichen or sheep,
a grazing horse or hobbled donkey.
Finisterre lighthouse looks after
the business of the sea;
beneficent, like all lighthouses,
it has one unbending purpose.
In the old and the new ends of town
the corn rows grow down
to the water between hotels,
and harbour-side townhouses.
The little green plants are upstanding.
There are no Realty views in this landscape;
there is the gorse and rock-strewn
headlands, there are the places
where people and livestock live,

there is granite and sand and forest
and farm and the grey waves that heed
only their unflagging momentum.

Cow, Galicia

We were leaning in silence on
the slim shadow of the stone byre
when she stirred herself
to pay attention to us,
or to ask us to pay attention
to her. The wall rumbled from within
with the effort of her weight and scramble
to lift her bulk on two hoofs.
I remember the dull thuds and scuffs
of her efforts and failures
sounding hollow in her empty cell;
and that she snorted great, warm breaths
once she had made it upright, and how
her soft mouth at the end of her long nose
just fitted in the small gap above us
where a stone had once been
and from which she tugged
the handfuls of thick grass blades from me.
Soon we would see her herd around the corner
each tear-streamed milking cow
secluded in a filthy concrete stall,
some in calf lying in their stench
and misery. I pictured the one
back down the road,
a lone cow in her dark cell,
thought of the effort she had made
in the dark, the effort she had made
to hold up that weight on two hooves

to take in the sunshine, the fresh green grass.
Most of all I remember her living black eye
letting in light, seeking out ours.

Muxia

The town of Muxia
holds out the encircling arms
of its breakwaters to cradle,
like a waiter with a big shiny tray,
the still waters of the marina
on which fishing tugs, yachts
and orange lifeboats balance.

An equilibrium of sorts: that calm
aloft on its tray while Muxia leans
back, intractable, shouldering the stone
from which her narrow lanes and houses
were chiselled and behind whose isthmus
the grey volume of the Atlantic
shoves and pounds through bedrock.

Visitation

I was on my hands and knees in the weeds
when they first appeared from behind the shed;
we were introduced at eye-level.

From that perspective the turkeys had the presence
of ostriches and their conversation
was a running stream over stones.

They moved like water too, muddy water,
glinting in sun, there were so many of them.
The crowd was composed of two families

each with its old patriarch like a high court judge
in his gown and wig, one all caramel and cream,
the other striped like a Plymouth

Barred Rock rooster. The chicks
looked to be the progeny of the former.
The hens meandered with minds of their own.

Odd that they should bear the moniker
of the gateway between East and West –
being a hallmark of their own vast continent.

Then one bird called to another in the queue to come and look,
at something new, their strange intelligence appraising
in those tiny heads while straining, it seemed, to supervise

their enormous bulk. The wire fences through which
they passed like water, were immaterial. The blue gum
the paddock, the clover and rye – we were all involved.

Lens

We were on the bridge
gazing into the marsh creek
whose waters, filtered by sedge
and ribbon grass and samphire,
threw light on the motion of worms
and the whims of small clams.
Somewhere in the landscape,
a harrier circled, a crane stooped,
each intent on its own business.
A short eel hovered in the current,
swallows dipped under the bridge
and back. Then from upstream
a bow-wave, pushed by a long gaze
that seemed to take us in:
two humans on a bridge.
Liquid, it looped, fur swaying
through figures of eight
ruddered by a narrow tail with
a white tip like a ring-tailed possum.
It snatched up a crab in small front paws
and with one motion was a creature
of the land whose supple, lean length
bent into a pot-hook
like a bandicoot but its feet
were half wading bird, half rodent.
The cracking of carapace and legs
revealed strong teeth. A comb
or two with the thin clawed toes
and the slate fur stood up softly
in air, mottled with auburn.

The water rat vanished as we blinked.
Since then, nothing much has changed;
the day's news, like any other's,
is filled with grief and fear and fury.
The water rat has not appeared again
under the wooden bridge
but the landscape is altered
beneath that cool, brackish lens.

First There, First Served

In the time lapse footage
of two runner beans
either side a pole
the first twin leaves on each
unfold, pulled out of air
as if by magic
while tips shoot
heavenwards at leisure,
each living string held vertical
as if by will.
A slow motion drama
gets underway.
The twin leaves flap
and brake – anchor, ballast,
effort, all as one;
the elongating shoots
become two angler's lines
or fine lassos, the pole between
becomes the stimulus and cue.
On either side the flailing tendrils
vie for purchase, while wing leaves
flap and bat the air.
At last the left plant strikes
the pole, and holds.
The effect is swift
upon the other runner bean
which halts its looping fly
and starts to die;
its whole self registers
despondency. Success

so palpably another's cost,
the plant has given up, all's lost.

Tyenna

A house by a river
might be idyllic
but how to stay in the present
beside a swift river –
Blackwood branches dipping,
stirring the rapids,
submerged grasses streaming
with the coursing rush,
clover straining to hold
its many faces above water –
they are out of their depth –
the tumult and the eddies
and the white specks
of foam rushing endlessly by
recalling the weeping philosopher.
The gamelan commotion!
the subliminal murmuring around stones,
the fluid imperative of elsewhere.

IV

Under the House

Dinner over, we changed into old clothes
to get on with the job under the house.
With pick-axe and shovel
we were excavating into the hill's gradient,
on the face of it to make another room.
Looking back, it *was* space he needed,
my father was suffocating in his new country.
We were at it for nights and months
and seasons – was it years? Like two miners,
a rigged up light bulb at the end of a long cord
hooked to a two inch nail. At the periphery
of its glow the light-starved grass
nearly touched the floorboards above.
A young girl, I grew strong on it: the night air,
swinging the axe, working the pick's nose
into fractures that levered into cracks –
columns of earth tottering
before the musty fall; the blade of the shovel
sharpening through loose mounds;
the taste of dry soil thick in the air
as his longing to be elsewhere. Above our heads
the distant sound of radio, television,
dishes clattering and voices
like airwaves from some distant planet.

The French Master

The French master wore
three-piece Harris tweeds.
In summer, when
the unabating northern sun
dulled us all to lethargy
he dispensed with jacket,
left the buttoned waistcoat on.
He had, for a young man in 1970,
old-fashioned style —
tailored trousers, well-cut shoes
in which he almost walked on tip-toe,
his life force shooting straight up
to high brow and shock
of Art Garfunkel hair. He taught me
all the grammar that I know;
declensions still come back
as if they're in my DNA.
On accent, he was pedantic
making clear that such things
mattered. Other things
were important too, like knowledge
and learning for everyone.
He'd fix the class
in his iris-ringed gaze.
I like to think
he was schooled in the dignity
and confidence of 1930's
departmental architecture
when public education's future
seemed assured. The day

the headmaster mustered the school
on the terraces for an extraordinary
assembly there was a breeze blowing.
I remember how it half wrapped him
in his academic gown.
Surely he didn't announce
the appalling particulars?
Perhaps we'd already heard...
the solitary walk into the bush,
the petrol can. Standing there
in our year groups
even the renegades fell quiet.
The headmaster in flapping gown
that slipped from his shoulder,
his glasses also askew,
looked as if he might have blown away.
The act of immolation...
the absence of pity. I was lucky,
I suppose, not to have encountered
hell before the age of thirteen.

Bede

From his narrow cell in Jarrow,
Bede restructured time and understood
the Earth was spherical. He knew of latitude,

and watched the influence of moon on tides
on quiet walks along Northumbrian coast.
Chronicles attest that in his life

men fought, were slain with axes,
tonsured, consecrated, exiled from the main.
Murder, theft, insult and punishment

were commonplace, then as now. Peacetime
was a litany of tool and trade, of net
and crook and hawk, each to their task.

While Bede, a man who loved good carpentry,
put his mind to history, philosophy
and science. In a world of ox and awl

and plough, Bede studied Plato,
Aristotle, music, poetry,
calculated movement of the stars.

His tireless hand, so frozen it could barely
grip the pen, described how maths
transcended the mundane, expanded matter.

Of migration tides from continental homelands
he had a modest vision
of a single people, language, nation

Music of the Spheres

Giordano Bruno 1548–1600

A slow jog
to the Campo on the mule;
between whose tall ears lies
the short route
that is the long distance
ahead. My hands are bound.
The flea-scratching curious
gather round the olive pyre;
and the dark unbending –
the figures of the Inquisition –
an impervious row of cypress.
Recant?
Could it, my iron-riven tongue
would tune exquisite heresies:
an infinite cosmos
of sun-centred worlds,
the mind at last acquainted
with its vastness, great and small:
this rancid smoke, the city's stones –
everything we see
and touch – worlds within worlds.
Even as the wood combusts
about my feet
the moving gladness of the cosmos
and its constellations sing.
Ashes and smoke;
love residing in the infinite elements.

Cyprus 1970

For WS

Rescued by her brothers
one morning from brutality,
she left a husband
(newly crippled)
and a house on the hill
to return to the village
of her parents
where she showed
a marvellous aptitude
for professional mourning:
gnashing, wailing,
tearing at her blouse
and her breast;
she filled a niche,
the need for solicitude
in public grief —
a raven-like figure
at gravesides
of abandonment
and thrilling lamentation.
Her reputation travelled far.
You recall how she'd pause,
composed,
from noisy protestations
and rent cloth
to respond to your boy's errand,
returning, as you retreated,
to the ciphering
of universal woe.

Her face in this photograph
you show me now, is mild, genial;
there is a lightness
about her that contrasts
with the gravity
of the big handed peasants
on either side.

Faces

What can we do with the faces
of the children of Aleppo and Mosul
who wear the blood and the dust of their lives
on their brows, in their unblinking eyes?

What can we do with the faces
of the schoolgirls of Chibok,
assembled not behind their teacher,
but behind a masked man with a gun

who stands, in turn, behind the sorrows
of the faces of mothers and fathers?
The old women, the old men
on the road to somewhere that's not home;

the faces of the fearful and the hungry
and the lost; and those who have lost hope at home
or in foreign countries of the present and past?
The heart beats from fright to fright.

After the letters and petitions, the credit cards,
what can we do with them all, those faces,
but carry them inside us like lesions.
or wear them outside like corsages on our hearts.

Hope

You told me a story,
years ago,
of miners trapped
by rock-fall;
a limited supply of air;
the man with the watch
who fibbed to his mates,
falsely reckoning
the hours of oxygen
remaining;
the other men believing
their hours passed
more slowly than
the sunlit world's above.
The time-keeper, you said,
was the only one who died
when the true hour came,
the oxygen minutes
trickling like sand
through an hourglass
in his mind.
The rest, who thought
they had more air,
more time,
were found alive.
You deny having heard
this story.
Was it a dream? It was
a metaphor, an allegory:
the silence of the dusty men,

the watch,
its square digits glowing
unambiguously in
the impenetrable dark,
if it worked at all.

Dahlia Show

(Dunalley)

Stripped of the untidiness of foliage,
there is only the perfection of each bloom,
each perfect flower's geometry. The blues

and greens have been erased from this white light
to leave a spectrum of such orange, pink
and yellow cheer the heart could burst

like these mandalas in their bottle rows,
fruit of each gardener's tender diligence.
The country hall's alight! the fibril reds,

the pompoms' pink munificence.
Each flower's complete, a universe.
That such loveliness be possible,

a mirror of a state attainable
in these unadulterated blooms eludes
all understanding. How a judge might choose
a winning form is anybody's guess.

Anachronisms II

I forgot to mention the tinkle
of the ice-cream van,
that peculiar suburban resonance,
like hand-bells on the wind,

threading the concrete curbs
and cul-de-sacs of memory
its tempo faltering
as if unwound by a turning handle.

This was before family-sized tubs,
or cheap boxed choc-ices,
or freezers bigger than glove-boxes.
The ice-cream van was a Pied Piper

mustering recalcitrant children
from backyards and streets
into ad hoc lines in its snail-paced
wake; a benign child-catcher

insinuating its pheromonal melody
through window glass and doors
ajar in consciousness and play.
It called out to all the senses

the way the red and yellow stripes
of the circus tent beckoned
as they bulged and undulated in a breeze,
guy ropes straining, like the lines

on a hot air balloon,
barely holding to earth
the sawdust and horse-dung smelling
magnitude of physical and fantastical potential.

The tinkling tune,
the billowing big-top –
the world shrunk or grown,
to a redolence of possibility.

V

The Grammar of Undoing

i

Parkinson's

And what I know is here – my breath, a table
and a chair, the sky, the morning light that brings
me to each day – an introduction as if
the first, each morning. What makes sense – a voice?
– a face? Sometimes these shaking hands.
Foliage makes sense of all of this, there is
a lexicon in trees, the leaves that catch
the wind assuring me of what I know. And truth
in children as I set the plates for tea.
Clap hands now Loves and ring the bell.
What's past is now, and what's now is gone.
Disease pulls me away, to light and dark.
I lose my way again. The children fade.
These shaking hands are all I have to guide me.

ii

The Garden

The first to go
was a pool of golden tradescantia
that glittered at the foot of the fig tree.
Inside the white bird netting
in the wind's hiatus
they bloomed in summer
like florist's arrangements.
Without them, the fig looked
emboldened, its grey skin trunk
sprouting masterfully from the green lawn.

The first sign that all was not right
was when she conceded the slow
erasure of her two-acre garden
for fifty years her peace,
her art and church.
She knew the provenance of each plant
she'd nurtured from the time
before the house stood,
when there was no garden
just an overgrazed, hard-bitten,
phosphated sheep paddock
by an antipodean river in a rain shadow.

The next bed, adjacent to the fig,
ran parallel to a crazy paving path
of dolerite and river stone.
The border was heralded
by dark-veined canna lilies
and yellow coreopsis.
Height, texture and colour gone,
the front lawn looked like a bowling green.

A couple of apple trees departed then:
a golden delicious and granny smith.
The back rose bed left a vacuum
in which ghosts of Papa Maillon,
Polar Star and the anonymous pink
from a garage sale lingered.

From the back window you could see

that the wind moved more freely

through the absences

that included the little rock roses
and daisies on the border;

                    the river stones

had also been removed.

Did the white mulberry go then?
– it had never come to much
as a bearer of fruit.

By this time, the vegetable beds,
raised on railway sleepers

and furnished with chicken wire
        to keep off possums and rabbits

    were vacant too;

they held their ground

but the rich compost was fallow.

            Around the side steps

    the species count dwindled
                    and in the long back flower bed

        even the oldest witnesses,
    the first exotic flowers to stake their claim
                    on the dry paddock fifty years before,
began to tire.

Those that held fast
were Blue Gum and Native Hop,
the shimmering Casuarina

she'd shake
    from spiky pods
        to germinate in drought.

My mother became quieter,

her tremulous hands
                took on a life of their own;

                        she spent
    more time indoors

    as the absences widened.

            In the gestalt of negative spaces

we started to see other shapes.

iii

The Grammar of Undoing

Your sentences balance subjects and objects;
each sentence still contains a verb but now
the doing may be anybody's guess.

In accordance with the rules your predicates
affirm your subjects every time
though nouns and adjectives are hit and mostly miss.

Tense, singular and plural all agree
this is a working system with
regular third person plural point of view.

But first person singular is out of mind,
is now impossible to find. Where has
the pronoun referring to the speaker gone?

It's the lexicon that lays bare the shift
we cannot parse, that shapes your altered space and time
or else implies a new ambivalence to signified and sign.

iv

Real Life

Called out in my pyjamas I find
your basket packed;
you're ready to go somewhere called Home.
I take you to the kitchen
where we make milo
and talk about the house
in which you lived for fifty years,
something in your urgency
suggests you're going further back.
You cling as if to a lifeline.
Somehow your husband
has become not that but multiples,
one of whom you loved and married,
the rest are a collective
or conspiracy.
We walk hand in hand
to your room. I switch on the light
and the electric blanket;
we unpack the basket together.
Then, it's gently out of the day clothes
and into the night.
You're patient while I do up each button
and fasten your dressing gown.
We return to a room
where a stranger is listening
to *Amazing Grace*.

The voice on the cassette recorder
is ringing with Nana Mouskouri's
tremolo emotion.
The stranger pats a chair.
You sit beside him keeping one eye
at all times on me.
Nana segues into *Time to Remember*.
My father's tenor
fashioned on Flanagan and Allen
during World War II joins in.
He leans on you, drawing you to lean on him.
You keep your wary eye on me, and smile
ironically. There you are now,
balalaika ringing from the winding reel,
Nana's mezzo quavering with his smooth resonance,
the rhymes so predictable:
remember and *tender*, *September* and *December*.

v

Lethe

…Our birth is but a sleep and a forgetting
                                        Wordsworth

She looks across the broad plane of the river,
like someone searching for a lost love,
beyond Canary Island palms to where,
upon the distant shore,
a mirage glints in autumn light.
Something in the sun dial of the Quoin,
and the sleeping mammal of Mt Direction
bear her gaze … a dim lit memory
of nearly half a century.
What comes to mind behind the captive gaze?
… filaments of Casuarina
etched against an unforthcoming sky…
a sheep fence running out across
the musseled river stones,
its rusty iron gate an invitation to
another point of view… And there,
a clothesline slung
between two aging wattle trees…
the love and labour of a billowing row of sheets
receding through the washing days of time
dimming into dark and distant space…
Does she recall the wakeful plover
calling through the dark?
Somewhere in the skyscraper blue gums

she planted is a dazzle of feasting lorikeets...
her signature rustles in the wallaby grass
that elms illuminate in golden light...
also in golden light, the ever present wraiths,
her grown up children in their infancy
who run and play and sit upon her bed
and move, unsettlingly, wherever brightness moves.

vi

Light

Your days, numbered then, seemed destined
to be textured by the black dog's barking
from the garden next door. A nuisance to begin with,
noi-sy...the two syllables floated without traction
inside the gentle breath of your sigh.
We were so busy at first looking for things to do:
adjusting, modulating, as if each twitch of the curtain
or dial on the heater, the sweetness or warmth of drinks
and whether you took them by teaspoon or dropper
or sponge made all the difference in the world.

Always, on the periphery of thought, the darkness
of the invisible dog barking, day and night,
through the window behind the fence.
We wrote notes. We knocked and pressed the doorbell.
Nobody but the dog seemed to be home
even when lights came on at night.
Who stopped minding it first – you? Or us?
The dog still barked, we felt its bass in our chests
but no longer heard nor entreated nor protested
as you, in those long last days
absorbed by the dog's deep shadow, finally touched clear light.

Acknowledgements

Some of these poems have appeared in the pages of *Australian Poetry Journal, Cordite, Griffith Review, The Best Australian Poems 2013,14,15,16 &17, The Australian, The University of Canberra VC Prize anthology 2015, The ACU Poetry Prize anthology 2016, Communion* online journal and *Antipodes.* The poems "Towards Light"; "big punchbowl"; "Middens" and "Eastern Curlew" were all written as part of the Bett Gallery & Tasmanian Land Conservancy Poets and Painters Project in response to the Big Punchbowl Reserve at Freycinet Peninsula, Tasmania.

Grateful acknowledgement is made to the Literature Board of the Australia Council for an Established Writers Grant and to Collegiate School, Hobart for a period of leave that enabled the completion of this book.

In "Towards Light": *The beautiful is limited but the sublime is infinite* comes from Kant's Critique of Judgement. "A Chicken's Head" is a pastiche of Miroslav Holub's "A Boy's Head". "Promises Promises" addresses the "World" persona in Thomas Hardy's poem: "He Never Expected Much". For further insights into the Eastern Curlew I'm happy to direct readers to the inimitable John Clarke's and Brian Dawes': "Farewell Shorebirds, Interview with an Eastern Curlew" on https:// www.youtube.com/watch

This book is dedicated in loving memory of my mother Margaret Day (1927-2015), to Carers and to researchers working on treatment for Parkinson's Disease.

Thank you to Gordon Harrison-Williams for his unswerving support and astute feedback and for his cover design and to our daughters for their insights and curiosity. Thanks to Janeil Hall too for her clarity and kindness, to Ruth Blair, Will Simon, Jean Page, Raymond Arnold and Graeme Hetherington for their thoughts and finally to Christopher Wallace-Crabbe, Janine Burke and John Kinsella for their generous time in reading this work.

www.ingramcontent.com/pod-product-compliance
Lightning Source LLC
Chambersburg PA
CBHW030848090426
42737CB00009B/1145